THE SCHOOLS HISTORY PROJECT
S·H·P
OFFICIAL TEXT

ESSENTIAL
THE STRUGGLE FOR PEACE IN
NORTHERN IRELAND

a modern world study

IAN DAWSON
BEN WALSH

Hodder Murray
A MEMBER OF THE HODDER HEADLINE GROUP

The Schools History Project

The Project was set up in 1972, with the aim of improving the study of history for students aged 13–16. This involved a reconsideration of the ways in which history contributes to the educational needs of young people. The Project devised new objectives, new criteria for planning and developing courses, and the materials to support them. New examinations, requiring new methods of assessment, also had to be developed. These have continued to be popular. The advent of GCSE in 1987 led to the expansion of Project approaches into other syllabuses.

The Schools History Project has been based at Trinity and All Saints College, Leeds, since 1978, from where it supports teachers through a biennial Bulletin, regular INSET, an annual Conference and a website (www.tasc.ac.uk/shp).

Since the National Curriculum was drawn up in 1991, the Project has continued to expand its publications, bringing its ideas to courses for Key Stage 3 as well as a range of GCSE and A level specifications.

Note: The wording and sentence structure of some written sources have been adapted and simplified to make them accessible to all students, while faithfully preserving the sense of the original.

Words printed in SMALL CAPITALS are defined in the Glossary on page 68.

Layouts by Amanda Easter
Artwork by Richard Duszczak, Tony Jones/Art Construction, Janek Matysiak, Tony Randell, Steve Smith
Cover design by John Townson/Creation

Typeset in 13/15 Berthold Walbaum by Fakenham Photosetting, Fakenham, Norfolk
Printed and bound in Italy

A catalogue entry for this title is available from the British Library

ISBN -10: 7195 7751 9
ISBN -13: 978 0 7195 77512

Acknowledgements

Photos
Cover © Reuters; **p.2** *t* Fotomas Index, *c* The Illustrated London News Picture Library, *b* photograph © Barney McMonagle/Guildhall Press; **p.3** *l* Belfast Telegraph Newspapers, *r* Mike Mahoney © Reuters; **p.5** *t* Belfast Telegraph Newspapers, *b* Martin McCullough/PA Photos; **p.15** *t* Mark Fenn/Camera Press, *b* Pacemaker Press; **p.17** *main & inset* popperfoto.com; **p.18** from *We Shall Overcome – The History of the Struggle of Civil Rights in Northern Ireland 1968–1978* (NICRA, 1978); **p.21** *l* Belfast Telegraph Newspapers, *r* photograph copyright Barney McMonagle/ Guildhall Press; **p.23** *l* Flash90/ASAP/Camera Press, *r* EPA/PA Photos; **p.28** *t* photo by Dr Jonathan McCormick, *b* Andy Butterton/PA Photos; **p.30** Source, *Drawing Support: Murals in the North of Ireland*, Belfast, Beyond the Pale Publications 1992, p.1; **p.37** *t & b* photograph © Barney McMonagle/Guildhall Press; **p.42** Source, *Drawing Support 2: Murals of War and Peace*, Belfast, Beyond the Pale Publications 1995, p.24; **p.47** Colman Doyle/Camera Press; **p.48** *t* Pacemaker Press, *c* Mark Fenn/Camera Press, *b* courtesy Lagan College, Belfast; **p.50** *t* Mike Mahoney © Reuters, *b* © Reuters; **p.51** *t* ROTA/Camera Press, *b* John Giles/PA Photos; **p.52** *tl* Neil Libbert/Camera Press, *r* © Reuters, *bl* Pacemaker Press; **p.53** *t* Neil Libbert/Camera Press, *b* Pacemaker/Camera Press; **p.54** *t* © Reuters, *b* Mark Fenn/ Camera Press; **p.55** Pacemaker Press; **p.56** *t* PA Photos, *b* Martin McCullough/PA Photos; **p.57** John Townson/Creation; **p.60** Pacemaker Press; **p.62** Mike Mahoney © Reuters; **p.66** EPA/PA Photos; **p.67** EPA/PA Photos.

(*t* = top, *b* = bottom, *l* = left, *r* = right)

Text
p.28 Extract from *Young Ned of the Hill*, The Pogues, Perfect Songs Ltd, Proper Music Publishing Ltd; **p.41** Peter Taylor, *The Provos: IRA and Sinn Fein*, Bloomsbury, 1998; **p.45** Source 2: Robert Harbinson, *No Surrender: An Ulster Childhood*, Faber, 1960, Source 3: Cal McCrystal, *Reflections on a Quiet Rebel*, Michael Joseph, 1997; **p.47** Brian Moore, *Lies of Silence*, Bloomsbury, 1990.

Every effort has been made to contact copyright holders, but if any have been inadvertently overlooked the publishers will be pleased to make the necessary arrangements at the earliest opportunity.

Contents

INTRODUCTION

1641

▼ **SOURCE 1**

Driuinge Men Women & children by hund:
reds vpon Briges & cafting them into Riuers,
who drowned not were killed with poles &
fhot with mufkets.

1914

▼ **SOURCE 2**

1969

▼ **SOURCE 3**

1976

▼ **SOURCE 4**

1998

▼ **SOURCE 5**

Caption A

Barricades put up by Catholics during the Battle of the Bogside in Londonderry

Caption B

The aftermath of a bomb in Omagh. The bomb killed 29 people. It was planted by an extremist group who were against peace talks

Caption C

A peace rally held in the People's Park, Ballymena

Caption D

A massacre during a rebellion in Ireland. Both Catholics and Protestants said that they were the victims of massacres

Caption E

UNIONISTS smuggling illegal weapons into Ireland. They were building up weapons so that they could fight to stop Ireland becoming independent

---

■ **DISCUSS**

Here are five pictures from Irish history and five captions.

1 Match each picture with its correct caption.
2 What impression do these pictures give you of the history of Northern Ireland?

Your questions

3 What questions about Northern Ireland do you want to find answers to in this Modern World Study? They could be questions about these pictures or they could be bigger questions about Irish history.

What is a Modern World Study?

MURDER IN OMAGH
The Guardian, 17 August 1998

Policing reform is badly needed
Sunday Independent, 11 January 2004

IRA man threatened to kill me – ex-Provo
Belfast Telegraph, 15 January 2004

New ban on parade for Bloody Sunday
Irish News, 30 January 2004

Irish dream of peace is fading
New York Daily News, 29 June 2001

The news is full of stories about violence and conflict. A Modern World Study looks behind those news stories. It helps you to understand **why** these things are happening.

This Modern World Study is about Northern Ireland. By the end we hope you will understand a lot about why there has been violence in Northern Ireland and why it has now become much more peaceful. But we also hope that the skills you learn – about looking at the history behind the news – will help you to understand other news stories a little better too.

■ ACTIVITY

As you work through this book collect your own newspaper headlines or articles about Northern Ireland. Include articles from the internet. Check news websites such as BBC News and BBC Northern Ireland, and check the websites of newspapers such as the *Belfast Telegraph, Belfast Newsletter, Irish News, Irish Times* and *Irish Independent*.

Your pathway

You won't study every event in Irish history. There isn't time. So we have selected one **big question**:

> Why has it been so difficult to have a lasting peace in Northern Ireland?

We have selected what we think are the most significant events to help you answer that question.

And here are three important skills that you will use in this Modern World Study:

Understanding causes – the complicated mixture of reasons that explain why things happen.

Comparing interpretations and understanding why the same events can be interpreted in different ways.

Using evidence and deciding which evidence to trust.

Chapter 1 What caused 'the Troubles'? Is it really all about religion?

You will find out why 'the Troubles' began in 1968.

Chapter 2 Does history really make peace more difficult?

You will examine events that took place 400 years ago that still make people angry today. But you will also discover that these events are not quite what they seem to be.

Chapter 3 Why don't the simple answers work?

You will study three attempts to stop the violence and find out why these solutions actually made the problem worse, not better.

1968 THE TROUBLES

Chapter 4 Why are fears and prejudices so strong?

You will work out why people who live in the same place have been so afraid of each other.

More death and hatred!

Chapter 5 Why should we be optimistic about peace?

You will examine some of the changes that took place in the late twentieth century.

Conclusion Why has it been so difficult to have lasting peace?

You will sort out your answers to our **big question**.

The next four spreads will help you get your bearings. You can also use them later if you need to check details.

Orientation 1: **Catholics and Protestants...**

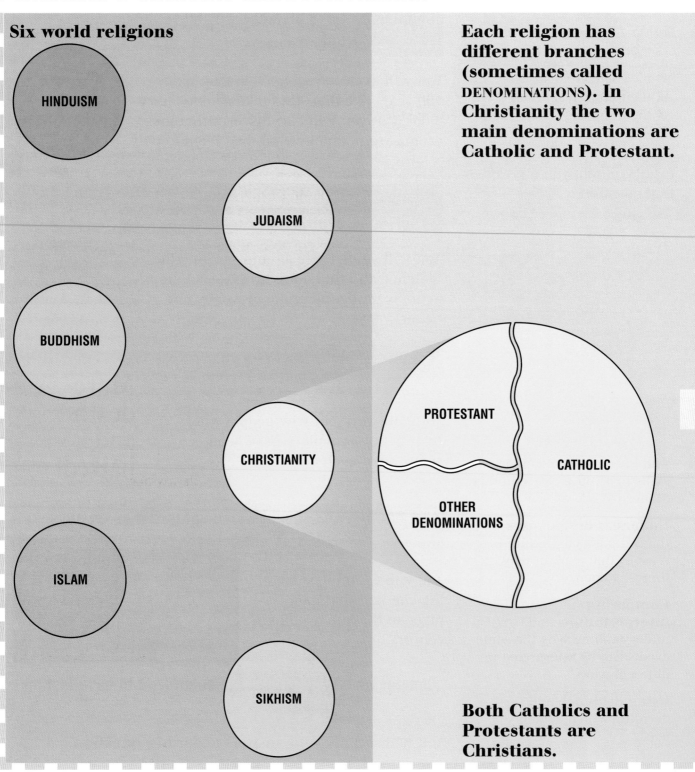

Six world religions

HINDUISM

JUDAISM

BUDDHISM

CHRISTIANITY

ISLAM

SIKHISM

Each religion has different branches (sometimes called DENOMINATIONS). In Christianity the two main denominations are Catholic and Protestant.

PROTESTANT

CATHOLIC

OTHER DENOMINATIONS

Both Catholics and Protestants are Christians.

...similarities and differences

In the Middle Ages all Christians were Catholics:

■ their leader was the Pope in Rome

■ their church services were in Latin

■ their churches were highly decorated.

But then some Christians decided that they did not like the way the Catholic Church was run. They protested that the Pope and his bishops were too wealthy and that the churches were too richly decorated. They protested that ordinary people could not understand the services because they were in Latin.

This happened around 1500. These people were called Protestants because of all their protests, and they set up a different form of Christianity called Protestantism. These events are known as the Reformation because the Protestants wanted to reform the way Christianity was practised. But they still worshipped the same God.

During the Reformation many Christians became Protestants:

■ their church services were in English

■ their churches were plainly decorated and their priests (often called ministers) wore simple robes

■ they tried to run their churches without bishops or other leaders.

After these changes some Christian countries stayed mostly Catholic. Some countries became mostly Protestant. Most countries had a mix of Catholics and Protestants.

Orientation 2: What happened when?
Your Irish history timeline

■ ACTIVITY

Your task is to sort out these events to create your own timeline of Irish history. Each event matches one of the dates on the timeline below.

a) Match blue cards A–D with numbers 1–4 on the timeline for 1500–1700.

b) Match red cards E–I with numbers 5–9 on the timeline for 1700–1922.

c) Match yellow cards J–O with numbers 10–15 on the timeline for 1922–2000 (see page 10).

You will need to read the details on the cards carefully. They contain lots of clues to help you work out the order. If there are any words here that you do not understand, refer to the Glossary on page 68.

A **1640s – rebellions and massacres**
Catholics rebelled because their land was given to new Protestant settlers. Catholics massacred Protestants, then Oliver Cromwell's Protestant army massacred Catholics.

B **In 1500 almost everyone in Europe belonged to the Catholic Church**
Therefore almost everyone in England and Ireland was Catholic.

C **Henry VIII turned England into a Protestant country**
Ireland stayed Catholic. English monarchs did not have a large enough army to force the Irish to change their religion.

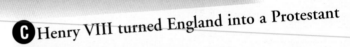

D **The Battle of the Boyne**
In 1688 two rivals fought to be crowned king of England – James (a Catholic) and William (a Protestant). Protestant William defeated Catholic James at the Battle of the Boyne, and became William III.

  1

  2

  3

  4

1500   1600   1700

E The Easter Rising

In the middle of the First World War Irish REPUBLICANS (people who wanted Ireland to be independent of Britain) took over parts of Dublin, hoping to force the British government to make Ireland independent. They failed.

F The Famine

The Irish potato crop failed. Millions of people in Ireland depended on potatoes for food. The British government was slow to help. Over a million Irish people starved to death. This led to many Irish people wanting HOME RULE (Ireland to rule itself rather than being ruled by Britain).

I The Act of Union

The British government closed the Irish Parliament in Dublin. From now on, Ireland was completely ruled from London.

G The Partition of Ireland

Just one year after the First World War there was another war in Ireland between the British government and Irish Republicans. To avoid further fighting Britain made a treaty with the Republicans that split Ireland into two parts. The Irish Free State became an independent country with 32 counties. The other six counties became Northern Ireland and remained part of Britain.

H Britain nearly decided to give Home Rule (independence) to Ireland

This almost led to a rebellion by Unionists (people who wanted Ireland to stay part of Britain) but the plan was postponed when the First World War began in 1914.

6

7 8 9

1900   1960

J **The arrival of the British army**
Northern Ireland seemed to be heading out of control after two days of rioting in Londonderry. The British government decided that the best way to bring peace was to send the British army to Northern Ireland to keep order.

K **The Good Friday Agreement**
In 1998 the British and Irish governments made a new agreement about the future of Northern Ireland. There was also an IRA ceasefire. These events led to the most peaceful period since 1968.

N **Direct Rule**
Violence increased, even after the army moved in to Northern Ireland. In 1972 the British government took over the government of Northern Ireland to try to solve the problems.

L **Internment**
Anyone suspected of terrorism was INTERNED – held in prison without trial. This was meant to stop the violence, but only Catholics were interned, so this led to another civil rights protest march in Londonderry in which thirteen marchers were shot dead by the army. This became known as **Bloody Sunday**.

M **Civil rights marches**
Marches were held to call for equal CIVIL RIGHTS for Catholics. The marchers said that in Northern Ireland Protestants were given the best jobs and the best housing. However, these marches led to violence when the protestors were attacked by Protestant PARAMILITARIES. This was the beginning of the Troubles – 30 years of violence.

O **Attempts at peace**
The British and Irish governments worked together to solve the problem of violence. In 1985 and 1993 they made agreements that seemed to get closer to peace.

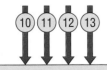
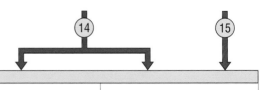

| 1960 | 1970 | 1980 | 1990 | 2000 |

Orientation 3: On the map! What is Northern Ireland?

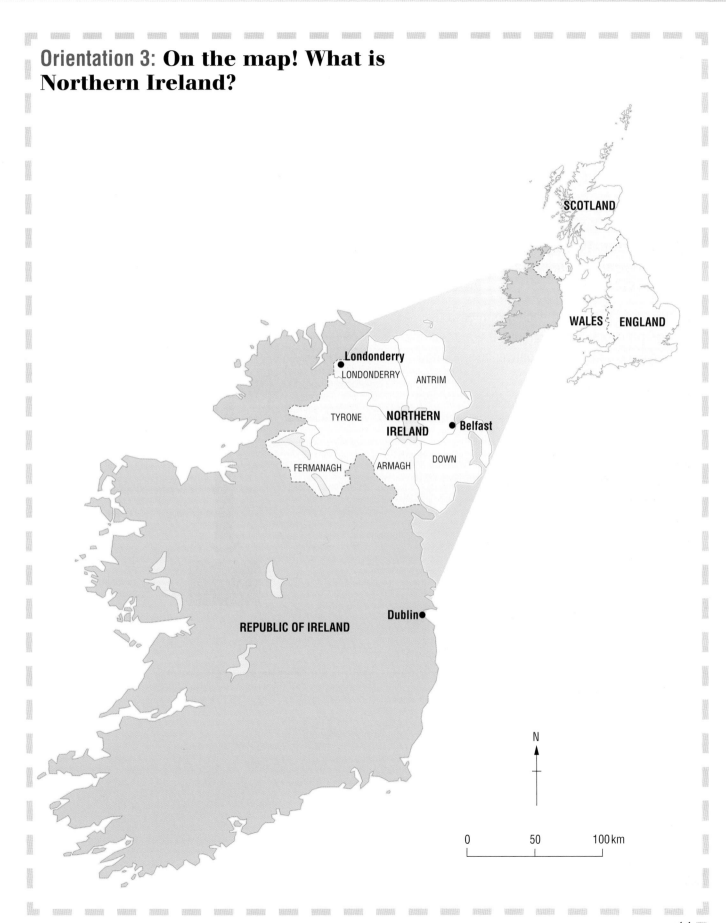

SCOTLAND

WALES   ENGLAND

Londonderry

LONDONDERRY   ANTRIM

TYRONE   **NORTHERN IRELAND**   • Belfast

FERMANAGH   ARMAGH   DOWN

REPUBLIC OF IRELAND

Dublin•

N

0   50   100 km

Orientation 4: **Who's who ... and what do they want?**

■ ACTIVITY

1 Here are four groups that you will hear about in your study of Northern Ireland.

   a) **Irish Republican Army (IRA)**
   b) ULSTER **Unionist Party (UUP)**
   c) **Ulster Volunteer Force (UVF)**
   d) **Social and Democratic Labour Party (SDLP)**

Your task is to put each group onto the graph (right). For example, if you think the group's aim is union between the United Kingdom and Ireland you would put it on the right side. If you think the group also uses violence to achieve this aim you would put it at the bottom on the right.

   Use the information opposite, about each group, to help you place it correctly. You could create your own version of this graph using a desktop publishing package.

■ RESEARCH

2 Find out who the leaders are of the groups listed above.

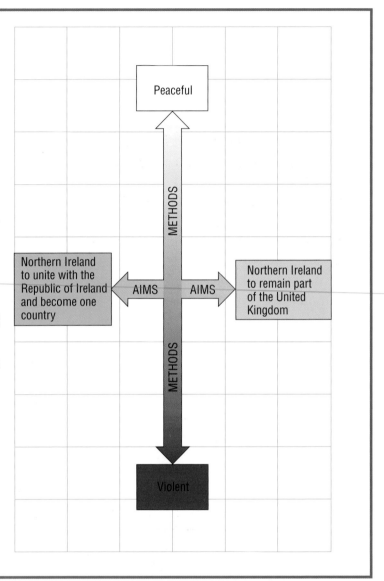

NATIONALISTS

- NATIONALISTS are mostly Catholic.
- Nationalists want one united nation called Ireland (which would include all of Northern Ireland). It should be independent from Britain.
- The most extreme Nationalists are often called Republicans.

POLITICAL PARTIES
Social and Democratic Labour Party (SDLP) – a democratic nationalist party that is strongly opposed to violence.
Sinn Fein – has close links with the IRA.

PARAMILITARY GROUPS
Irish Republican Army (IRA) strongly supports Northern Ireland breaking away from Britain and becoming part of the Republic of Ireland. It has often used violence against its opponents.

    The **Real IRA** and the **INLA (Irish National Liberation Army)** are groups that broke away from the IRA when the IRA started to agree peace.

ALLIANCE PARTY
The Alliance Party is a moderate unionist party which tries to win support from people of all religions and backgrounds.

UNIONISTS

- Unionists are generally Protestants.
- Unionists want to keep the union between Britain and Northern Ireland.
- The most extreme Unionists are often called LOYALISTS.

POLITICAL PARTIES
Ulster Unionist Party (UUP) – a democratic party that wants to keep Northern Ireland united with Britain. It is against the use of violence.

    Democratic Unionist Party (DUP) – a more hardline, but still democratic, party.

PARAMILITARY GROUPS
Ulster Volunteer Force (UVF) strongly supports Northern Ireland staying united with Britain. It has often used violence against its opponents.

    Ulster Freedom Fighters (UFF) – a splinter group of the UVF. They use violence to achieve their aims.

CHAPTER 1

What caused 'the Troubles'?
Is it really all about religion?

In this chapter you will study the start of 'the TROUBLES'. This is the name given to the violence that began in Northern Ireland in 1969 and which continued for over 30 years. During this time over 3600 people were killed in Northern Ireland. In this chapter you will investigate what caused the Troubles. In particular you will think about whether the Troubles are all about religion or whether the causes are more complicated than that.

This chart shows the number of deaths from violence in Northern Ireland since 1969. It can be hard to take in the reality of these numbers so try thinking of them as classes of students in your school. How many classes died in 1972? The total in 1998 is much lower but it is still two large classrooms full of people.

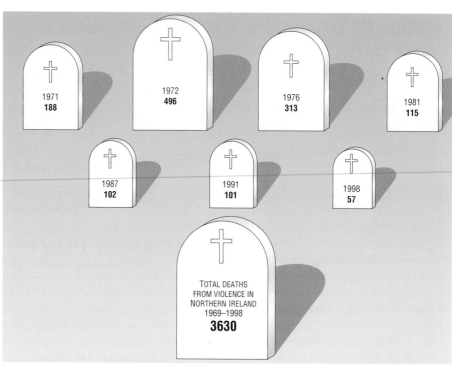

1971
188

1972
496

1976
313

1981
115

1987
102

1991
101

1998
57

TOTAL DEATHS
FROM VIOLENCE IN
NORTHERN IRELAND
1969–1998
3630

▲ **SOURCE 1** The number of people killed in the Troubles, 1969–1998

If you ask people in Britain what they think caused the Troubles a common answer might be:

I think it's all about religion. It's Catholics against Protestants isn't it!

This is a tempting idea. One side is mostly Protestant and the other side is mostly Catholic, so it would be easy to assume that it was religion they were fighting about.

■ DISCUSS

1 Look at Sources 2 and 3, below, and read the captions.
- **a)** What clues suggest that **religion was a cause** of the violence?
- **b)** Are there any clues that suggest **other causes** for the violence?

2 What clues in the timeline on pages 8–10 suggest the conflict is about religion?

3 Find out what ideas your class has. Take a class vote, using the ballot paper below.

Religion is **the only cause** of violence in Northern Ireland.	
Religion is **the major cause** of violence in Northern Ireland, but there are others.	
Religion is **a minor cause** of violence in Northern Ireland.	

► **SOURCE 2** Enniskillen, 1987. An IRA bomb went off at the Remembrance Day service. Eleven people, nearly all of them Protestants, were killed and over 60 were seriously injured

► **SOURCE 3** A bar in Loughinisland, County Down, after an attack by gunmen in 1994. Loyalist paramilitaries shot dead six Catholics who were watching a football match in the bar. It was one of a series of 'tit-for-tat' killings in the early 1990s

Why did the civil rights protests begin in 1968?

In 1968 Northern Ireland had been mostly peaceful for more than 30 years. However, this did not mean that everyone was happy. Many people were angry about the discrimination they faced in their everyday lives. As a result, the Northern Ireland Civil Rights Association (NICRA) was set up. Its leaders were mainly Catholics, but many ordinary Protestants also supported it when they realised the amount of prejudice experienced by Catholics.

■ ACTIVITY

1 The diagram below shows eight complaints that NICRA made about civil rights in Northern Ireland. Copy and complete the table by placing each of the complaints, A–H, in the correct column.

Jobs	Police	Voting	Housing

2 Explain whether each complaint seems to be linked to religion.

H Local councils were not fair in the way they provided housing. Two-thirds of houses built since 1945 had been given to Protestants.

A Catholic-led councils discriminated against Protestants in allocating housing. In Catholic-run Newry, Protestants were given only 22 out of 765 council houses.

G The part-time police, the B-SPECIALS, were nearly all Protestants, and had a bad reputation for violence against Catholics.

B Some large companies employed very few Catholics. The Harland and Wolff shipyard had 400 Catholics out of 10,000 workers.

F Only householders could vote in elections and people who had two houses or a house and a business property could vote twice. Protestants owned more of the businesses so they had more votes.

Complaints about civil rights in 1968

C There were few Catholics in the Civil Service and it was difficult for them to get promotion.

E The RUC (Royal Ulster Constabulary) had six times as many Protestant police as Catholics. This was partly due to discrimination, but extreme Republicans also discouraged Catholics from joining the police force.

D In Londonderry the election areas for the council were fixed to make sure as many Unionists as possible were elected. Around 9000 Protestants had twelve councillors whereas 14,000 Catholics had only eight councillors.

There were other reasons why people supported NICRA and joined the civil rights marches. Some of the most important reasons had nothing to do with Northern Ireland at all.

■ DISCUSS

Why would each of the three developments below help to encourage protests in Northern Ireland?

Civil rights protests in the USA
Peaceful protests and demonstrations, led by Martin Luther King, forced the US government to pass the Civil Rights Act outlawing discrimination on the grounds of colour and race.

②

Student demonstrations around the world
• In the USA there were massive student protests against the USA's involvement in the war in Vietnam.
• In London there were more student protests against the war in Vietnam.
• In Paris, student protests against government policies led to serious violence.

③

These events were seen on TV screens around the world
In 1958 only 9 million households in Britain had televisions. By 1968 this figure had increased to over 15 million.
So ordinary people saw far more about events all over the world.

How did peaceful protests lead to the beginning of the Troubles?

June 1968 – the Dungannon sit-in

The Dungannon Council gave a council house to a single Protestant woman who worked for a member of the Unionist Party, ahead of a Catholic family with children. Austin Currie was the local Nationalist MP and a NICRA supporter. He thought this was typical of the discrimination going on at that time. He decided to stage a sit-in. He occupied the house and demanded the council give it to the Catholic family as they had more need for it. The protest ended when police removed Mr Currie. But his actions received a lot of press and TV coverage.

August 1968 – the civil rights march, Coalisland to Dungannon

Currie suggested NICRA took further action so in August, 2500 marchers protested about discrimination against Catholics. They carried placards saying 'One Man, One House, One Job' and 'Jobs on Merit'. Police stopped the marchers from holding a meeting in Dungannon. But there was no violence.

▲ **SOURCE 4** The start of the first civil rights march in Coalisland, 1968

June 1968   **August 1968**

November 1968 – government reforms

There were more demonstrations throughout November and December. In reaction the government of Northern Ireland, led by Terence O'Neill, passed a series of reforms. The most important reforms were:

- council housing had to go to the neediest families first, whatever their religion

- the Londonderry council was suspended because of the unfairness of the city's voting system which ensured that Unionists controlled the city council.

The government also said it *would think about* introducing one person, one vote (rather than allowing only house-owners to vote). However, the government did not make any changes at that time.

October 1968 – the civil rights rally, Londonderry

A big march and meeting was planned to take place in Londonderry, but it was banned by the Northern Ireland government. This time the marchers ignored the ban and tried to get into the centre of Londonderry. The RUC stopped them crossing a bridge into the city and fighting broke out. Police officers used water cannon to stop the marchers and beat unarmed protestors with their batons.

January 1969 – the People's Democracy march

In January, 40 students began a three-day march from Belfast to Londonderry to protest that O'Neill's reforms had not gone far enough. Other protestors joined them. On the third day the marchers were ambushed by a loyalist mob at Burntollet Bridge near Londonderry. Bricks, bottles and stones were thrown by Loyalists (some of whom were off-duty police officers), they then beat the protestors with iron bars and sticks. The RUC police did little to protect the marchers. This violence is usually seen as the start of the Troubles.

October 1968

January 1969

Why was the reaction to the marches so violent?

The attack on the People's Democracy march in January 1969 was a turning point. Violence soon spread throughout Londonderry into other parts of Northern Ireland. There were bomb explosions (which were first blamed on the IRA, but were later found to have been caused by loyalist paramilitaries). Eighteen people were killed in 1969; each one was felt as a great shock in a country that had been peaceful for so long.

> ### ■ ACTIVITY
>
> On this page there are four reasons to explain why there was a violent reaction to the marches. Match each reason to one of the sources on the opposite page.

A Deliberate provocation by the marchers

There had been marches in Northern Ireland for many years by both Nationalists and Unionists, such as the Orange Order. They often deliberately set out to insult or provoke the opposition. Many believed the civil rights marchers were no different.

B Working-class Protestant resentment

Many working-class Protestants resented the marchers' demands. They said that they had the same problems as Catholics, for example unemployment and poor housing.

Why was the reaction to the marches so violent?

C Police attitudes

Religious discrimination in the police force was a long-term grievance for the civil rights campaigners.

D Unionist fear of the IRA and Republicanism

Many Protestants believed that the marches were organised by the IRA. Historians now know that at the time the IRA was very weak and had very little support. But during this period people believed the IRA was a strong influence.

▼ **SOURCE 5** A Protestant housewife's opinion of the civil rights movement, 1969

It was all the Catholics this, the Catholics that, living in poverty and us lording it over them. People looked around and said, 'What, are they talking about us? With the damp running down the walls and the houses not fit to live in.'

▲ **SOURCE 6** A demonstrator being hit by RUC officers at a civil rights rally in October 1968. The government's report into the violence criticised many Protestant police officers for violence against the marchers. The report said that 'A number of policemen were guilty of misconduct which involved assault and battery, damage to property.'

▲ **SOURCE 7** A civil rights march in Great James' Street, Londonderry. Nationalists deliberately planned a route through Protestant areas. Some of the marchers believed they were copying the famous civil rights marches in the USA, when black protestors marched through areas dominated by whites

▼ **SOURCE 8** From a speech by Ian Paisley, a Unionist leader, in January 1969

The civil rights people don't believe in civil rights at all, they're just a bunch of Republican rebels, that's what they are. Let's be very clear about this, they have no time for law and order, they have no time for this country and they mean to destroy this country, and we mean to see that this country will not be destroyed.

Review: so, is it just about religion?

By now you have collected a lot of evidence about the causes of the Troubles. It should be clear to you that it is about a lot more than religion.

The **big idea** in this chapter is:

There is not just one reason for the violence. There are several reasons and they are all mixed together.

The reasons

■ ACTIVITY

On a sheet of paper, write your own speech bubble to explain the causes of the violence. Make it as long as you like.

It may look like it is about religion because it is Catholics against Protestants, but look inside and you find...

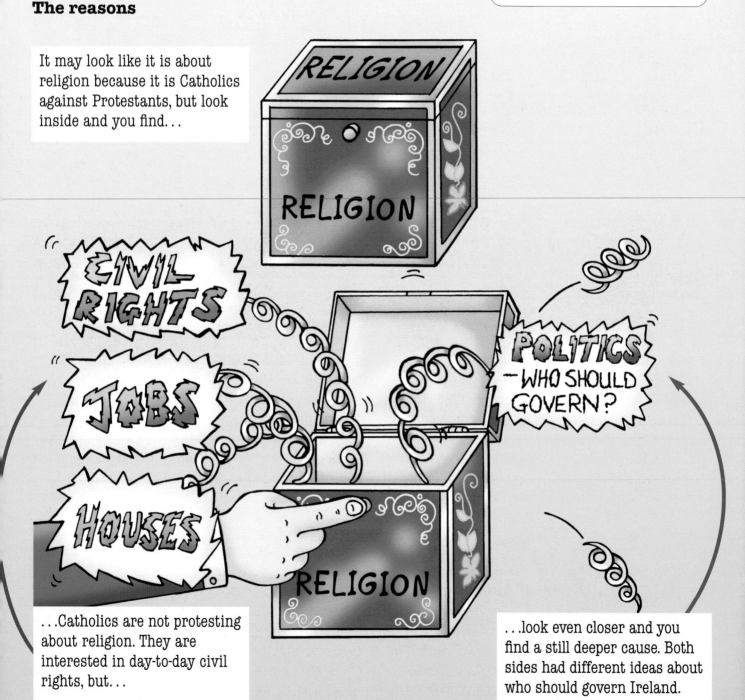

...Catholics are not protesting about religion. They are interested in day-to-day civil rights, but...

...look even closer and you find a still deeper cause. Both sides had different ideas about who should govern Ireland.

Why is this big idea so important?

If people think that there is just one reason for a problem, then they usually think that finding an answer should be simple. However, you know that there are several reasons, which are all tangled together. So finding an answer won't be simple.

 using the big idea

SOURCE 1 In the West Bank town of Ramallah, Palestinians throw rocks at Israeli troops, 2004

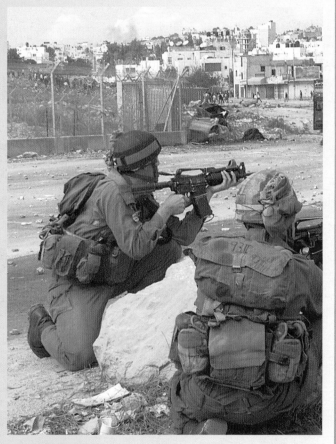

SOURCE 2 Israeli soldiers aiming at Palestinian protestors near the West Bank town of Ramallah, October 2000

What's in the news this week? Is there a story about violence in Britain or in another part of the world, such as the Middle East? Can you use what you have learned about Northern Ireland to think about another example of violence today where people say 'It's all about religion'?

1 What is the news story?
2 Why do you think religion is blamed for this problem?
3 What other reasons might there be for this problem?

CHAPTER 2   *Does history really make peace more difficult?*

Have you ever heard anyone say something like this?

Have you thought it yourself? If you live in England there's a good chance that you have. However, it is less likely if you live in Northern Ireland. People are very interested in history. In fact they are so interested in history that sometimes it becomes a problem!

> Why do I have to study Irish history? It's got nothing to do with me.

An Irish historian, Anthony Stewart, said: 'To the Irish … the past is simply a convenient quarry which provides ammunition to use against enemies in the present.'

In this chapter you will examine three different stories from Irish history and find out how people today use this history. This will help you with the **big question** for this chapter:

> Does history really make peace more difficult?

Who killed whom in the massacres of the 1640s?

In the 1640s there were massacres in Ireland. It is your job to work out who was killed and why.

A reporter has been sent to Ireland to find out about the massacres in the 1640s. She meets two people.

■ DISCUSS

1 How do the speakers in Interviews 1 and 2 disagree?
2 What do they agree on?
3 Do you think they could both be right?

Interview 1

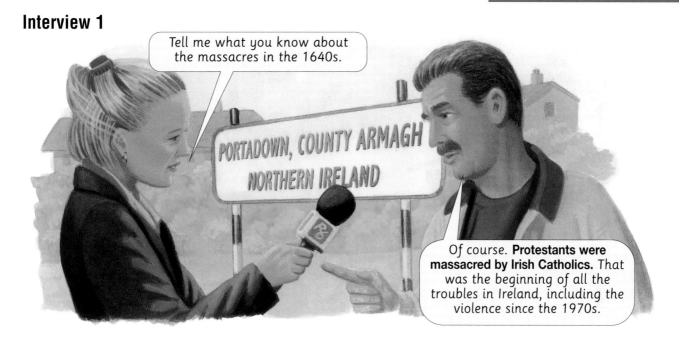

Interview 2

What really happened?

In the Middle Ages nearly everyone in England and Ireland was Catholic.

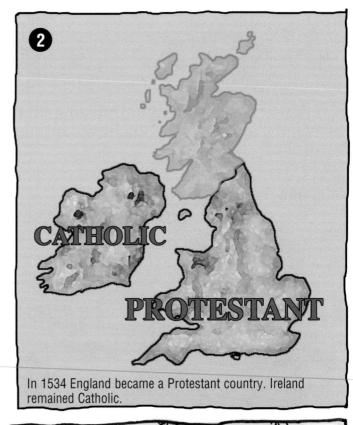

In 1534 England became a Protestant country. Ireland remained Catholic.

English rulers could not force the Irish to change their religion. And they did not try to. But they were worried that some of England's Catholic enemies, such as Spain, might use Ireland as a base to invade England. So...

...English monarchs sent Protestant farmers and traders over to Ireland.

The English monarchs took land away from the Irish Catholics and gave it to the Protestant settlers. The English hoped that if there were enough powerful Protestants in Ireland this would stop Catholic countries using Ireland as a base for invasion.

The Catholics became increasingly angry about losing their land. In 1641 the Catholics attacked the Protestant settlers. They killed between 2000 and 3000 Protestants.

Protestant propaganda exaggerated the massacres. One report said that over 150,000 people had been murdered. In 1649, Oliver Cromwell and his soldiers read and believed the propaganda about the massacre of Protestants in 1641.

In 1649, Cromwell took his army to Ireland and massacred thousands of Catholics. Many others were forced to leave their farms and move to poor, rocky land where farming was difficult.

■ DISCUSS

1 Look back at the two interviewees on page 25. Who was right about the massacres?
2 Why do you think these events might make peace more difficult today?

'Street history' versus 'real history'

'Street history'

Street history is the view of the ordinary person. It often involves selecting the bits of history which fit the story the writer wants to tell, and leaving out other bits. Street history is not the whole story.

THE PERSECUTION OF THE PROTESTANT PEOPLE BY THE CHURCH OF ROME 1600 THE ETHNIC CLEANSING STILL GOES ON TODAY

▲ **SOURCE 1** A mural in the Shankill area of Belfast, photographed in 2000. Northern Ireland has become famous for its murals. They are literally 'street history'. They appear in almost every area of Northern Ireland, particularly in Belfast. They show the history and political views of both communities and are a way of marking territory. They remind people that they are in a loyalist or a republican area

▼ **SOURCE 2** Part of a song written by Shane MacGowan in 1989. MacGowan was the lead singer of a band called 'The Pogues'. His songs were very popular

A curse upon you, Oliver Cromwell
You who raped our Motherland
I hope you're rotting down in Hell
For the horrors that you sent
To our misfortunate forefathers
Whom you robbed of their birthright
… may you burn in Hell tonight!

■ DISCUSS 1

Compare Sources 1 and 2 on page 28.

1 Summarise the message each source is trying to get across. Use only one sentence for each source.
2 Who do you think is the intended audience for each source – their supporters or their opponents?

'Real history'

Real history tries to tell the whole story. It is as unbiased as possible. It tries to give a more complete picture; to tell the truth however hard that might be. What does real history have to say about the massacres of the 1640s?

■ In 1641 the Catholics had a clear reason to rebel. They resented the fact that their land had been taken away from them to give to the new Protestant settlers. This explains what they did, but it does not justify it.
■ Between 2000 and 3000 Protestants were killed. However, Protestant propaganda exaggerated the total. One report said that over 150,000 people had been murdered.
■ In 1649 Cromwell and his soldiers read and believed the propaganda about the massacre of Protestants in 1641. This explains what they did, but it does not justify it.
■ There were many religious wars in Europe in the 1500s and 1600s and massacres like these were common. These massacres were terrible, but they were not unusual.

In real history we do not just believe what sources like Sources 1 and 2 show or say. We ask questions to find out whether the author of the source was biased against one side or the other.

■ DISCUSS 2

3 How does the real history of the 1640s differ from the street history? Make a list of the differences.
4 Using the massacres of the 1640s as an example, explain why street history might make peace more difficult.

Has it always been Catholic versus Protestant?

Now you can test another example of street history. Street history says that the fighting has always been Catholics against Protestants – so it will always be Catholics against Protestants. Is this right? You will investigate two stories – the first about a loyalist hero, William of Orange, and the second about a republican hero, Wolfe Tone – and draw your own conclusions.

Case study 1: The story of King Billy

▲ **SOURCE 1** A loyalist mural in Londonderry celebrating William III's arrival at the siege

---

■ ACTIVITY

1 Which information from the story-strip captions on page 31 would 'Street History Man A' choose to support his interpretation of history?

2 Which information would 'Street History Man A' ignore because it contradicts his interpretation of history?

3 Why might the mural in Source 1 make peace more difficult to achieve?

In 1690 the Protestants beat the Catholics at the Battle of the Boyne. It has always been Protestants against Catholics.

STREET HISTORY MAN A

The background

In 1688 England was ruled by a Catholic – King James II. Protestant nobles rebelled against James. They deposed him and asked a Protestant called William of Orange to be king. He became King William III. James tried to win back the English crown. He invaded Ireland, hoping that it would be a good base for invading England. James had success to start with. Then he reached Londonderry...

The events

The city of Londonderry looked easy. It looked as if James would just have to walk in without any resistance. But at the last moment thirteen apprentice boys shut and barred the city gates.

A long siege followed from April to July 1689. Londonderry's citizens suffered terribly, but they held out and in doing so became part of Protestant legend.

The siege of Londonderry gave William enough time to bring his forces to Ireland. William was a Protestant but many of his troops were Catholics sent by Pope Alexander (head of the Catholic Church).

William's army arrived at Londonderry and drove James' army away. William then defeated James at the Battle of the Boyne in July 1690.

Treaty

1. 15,000 of James' soldiers can go safely to France.
2. Catholics in Ireland can keep their lands if they promise to be loyal to William.
3. No extra limits on Catholics' freedom to worship.

The war was officially ended with the Treaty of Limerick in 1691. This was a generous treaty as William did not want to persecute the Catholics. His battle was against James, as his rival for the crown. It was not against the Catholics. He was more interested in fighting his wars in France than in the goings on in Ireland.

One hundred years later there was a parade to remember the Battle of the Boyne. Lots of Catholics, including the local Catholic bishop, joined the parade.

Case study 2: the story of Wolfe Tone

Catholics have always had to fight for their freedom and to have their own country. It was the same in the 1790s when Wolfe Tone led a rebellion against the English. You see, it's always been Catholics against Protestants.

STREET HISTORY MAN B

■ ACTIVITY

1 Which information boxes would 'Street History Man B' choose to support his interpretation of history?
2 Which information boxes would 'Street History Man B' ignore because they contradict his interpretation of history?

1 In the 1790s Wolfe Tone led campaigns to win Catholics the same rights as Protestants. For example, he wanted Catholics as well as Protestants to be able to vote, become MPs and army officers, to own land and to get a good education.

2 Tone led a rebellion by the United Irishmen against English rule in 1798. They received help from France, but the rebellion failed.

3 Wolfe Tone was a Protestant.

4 Tone wanted to bring all Irish people together, whatever their religion. He said 'My methods were to unite the whole people of Ireland, to abolish the memory of all past disputes, and to replace names like Protestant and Catholic with the name of Irishman.'

5 Tone was captured after the rebellion and sentenced to death. He committed suicide in prison in November 1798. He died for Ireland.

6 Tone began his career as a lawyer. He was reluctant to rebel and wanted to avoid violence. He used violent rebellion as a last resort when other methods had failed.

7 The United Irishmen included Catholics and Protestants. During the rebellion many Protestants, especially in Northern Ireland, fought against the British army.

8 Tone did not become a nationalist hero until the 1890s, 100 years after his death.

Review: does history really make peace more difficult?

Why do we have to study history? It's to stop street history taking over and spreading hate and violence.

The **Big idea** in this chapter is:

It's not history that's the problem. It's the way people use it!

■ ACTIVITY

Work in small groups. Your task is to write a short report advising the governments of Northern Ireland and the Republic of Ireland on the following question:

Why is it important for students in schools in Northern Ireland and the Republic of Ireland to study Irish history?

Your report should include five main paragraphs:

Paragraph 1   Describe an example of street history

Paragraph 2   Explain why this street history could lead to hatred of other people or to violence

Paragraph 3   Describe how the real history of this event is different

Paragraph 4   Explain why the real history could stop or reduce hatred and violence

Paragraph 5   Sum up your answer to the question 'Why is it important for students in schools in Northern Ireland and the Republic of Ireland to study Irish history?' in a conclusion. You could present your conclusion in a PowerPoint presentation.

---

 using the big idea

Is school History real history or can it be more like street history?

1 How many years of German history is this student studying?

2 What ideas about Germany might she develop?

3 What is she **not** studying about Germany?

4 In 2003 the German ambassador to Britain complained that British schools are spending too much time focusing on Nazi Germany. He argued that this encourages prejudiced attitudes towards Germany. Do you think he was right to complain?

5 Can you think of any other examples where street history spreads hatred or violence?

I'm studying modern German history, 1914–1945.

CHAPTER 3 *Why don't the simple answers work?*

Whenever there's a problem reported on the news, many of us will say something like:

Why don't they just . . .

The people below are saying the same thing about Northern Ireland. They are coming out with some of the simple, obvious answers that most of us have thought or said at one time or another.

. . . imprison the paramilitaries

. . . share the land between them

. . . send in the army

The trouble is that with a complicated issue like Northern Ireland the simple, obvious answers aren't always the best ones. That's why the **big question** in this chapter is:

Why do the simple, obvious answers often make peace more difficult?

1922 – Why didn't splitting Ireland in two work?

Now for the first obvious answer – splitting Ireland in two, one part for the Nationalists, one part for the Unionists. That's what happened in 1922. Now it's your turn to role-play that decision and assess whether it was the right one.

■ ACTIVITY

1 It is 1922 and you have to negotiate the future of Ireland. Work in groups of three. One of you is a Nationalist, one a Unionist and one a member of the British government. Decide who has which role.

2 Now come away from your groups so that all the Nationalists in the class meet together, and all the Unionists, and all the members of the British government.
Decide:
a) What your group wants to achieve

b) Whether you would accept a compromise, and if so, what? Use the page opposite to help you.

3 Now go back into your groups of three. Your task is to negotiate between you to decide on the future of Ireland. Use your answers to question 2 to help you. **You have to reach a decision**.

4 Each group should take it in turns to announce its decision to the whole class. What is the most popular decision – and why?

In 1916 some extreme Nationalists joined a rebellion known as the Easter Rising. They took over parts of Dublin, hoping to win independence for Ireland. The small British army in Ireland suppressed the Easter Rising in just a week but this uprising led to more rebellions against Britain. When the First World War ended in 1918, Britain was exhausted by the conflict, but still had to fight a war against the IRA, who used GUERRILLA tactics, until 1921. In Ulster alone 500 people were killed.

■ DISCUSS

Did either the Nationalists or the Unionists want Ireland to be partitioned?

Did the Partition of Ireland make peace more difficult?

1921

In 1921 the Republicans and the British government came to an agreement and the Anglo-Irish Treaty was signed. This was followed by the Partition of Ireland in 1922.

The Anglo-Irish Treaty 1921

1930

- Talks led to the Partition of Ireland.
- The Irish Free State was set up as an independent country with its own government.
- Ulster stayed part of Britain, ruled from London.
- This division (see Source 2) meant that many Catholics were living in Northern Ireland. They were a minority as the majority were Protestants.
- There were also many Republicans living in Northern Ireland. They were also a minority as the majority were Unionists.

1940

- Many Nationalists refused to accept the new state or to co-operate in its government. This led many Unionists to fear them as a potential enemy within. This in turn led to discrimination in some areas such as jobs.

■ DISCUSS

1. Why did Partition seem like a good idea to the British government in 1922?
2. Why was the border drawn where it was?
3. Why were
   a) Nationalists and
   b) Unionists
   unhappy with the treaty?
4. Did the simple answer – splitting Ireland in two – work? Explain your answer. (Make sure you study the timeline on the left of this page before you answer.)

1950

▼ **SOURCE 1** The Partition of Ireland, 1922

1960

▼ **SOURCE 2** Percentages of Catholics in the counties of Ulster, 1922

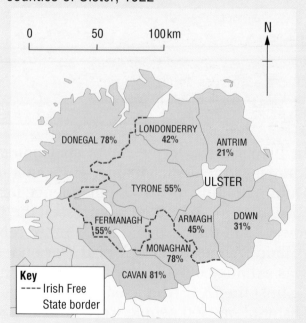

1968 THE TROUBLES

1970

1969 – Should the British army be used to keep peace in Northern Ireland?

Now for another tricky decision. 1969 saw riots, violence, houses burning down. The police had lost control. What would you have done next?

Date: August 1969

Place: The Bogside, a Catholic area of Londonderry

Events:

- Two days of rioting between Catholics and Protestants.

- Barricades and missiles made it impossible for the police to get into the area.

- At the same time there was rioting in Belfast. Houses were burned down. Around 1800 families were forced out of their homes – 1500 of them were Catholic.

- The police had lost control and there was a danger of the rioting spreading across Northern Ireland.

- The police were accused of bias in their harsh treatment of Catholics during the riots.

The decision: Should the British army be used to restore order?

▲ **SOURCE 1** Youths making petrol bombs in the Bogside, August 1969

▲ **SOURCE 2** Barricades in the Bogside, August 1969

■ DISCUSS

1 Can you think of two arguments for and against using the army on the streets of Northern Ireland to restore order?

2 What would you have chosen to do? What is the main reason for your choice?

1969 – what happened next?

Why should we use the army to
restore order?

- The police have lost control.
- The army is the only chance of
  restoring order quickly.
- The army is not biased.
- The army will protect everyone,
  Catholics and Protestants,
  against violence.

Using the army had unexpected consequences.

- The army was welcomed by the Catholic community at first but ...
- ... in the summer of 1970, after the murders of four Protestants, the
  Unionist government of Northern Ireland sent the army to search
  the Catholic Falls Road area. This was against the army's advice.
  People were not allowed to leave their homes for 35 hours and tear
  gas was used to keep order. Suddenly the army looked like the
  enemy to many Catholics.
- This helped the Provisional IRA win support. Until this point the
  IRA had received very little support because it did not do anything
  to defend the Catholic population. Now the Provisionals said that
  they could defend the people against the army.
- Support for the IRA increased in the USA because it looked as if the
  British army had taken over Northern Ireland.
- It was impossible for the British government to order the army out
  of Northern Ireland without it looking like a defeat.

■ DISCUSS

1 Explain in your own words what the phrase 'unexpected
  consequences' means.
2 Do you think that using the army was a good or a bad decision at
  that moment?
3 What were the unexpected consequences of using the army?
4 Did the simple answer – using the army – make peace more
  difficult? Explain your answer.

1971 – How can the paramilitaries be stopped?

Now you know that sending in the army did not bring peace. Instead, the violence increased. You must decide what you would have done next to try to stop the paramilitaries from operating in Northern Ireland.

The situation

1969
10 people were killed and 154 suffered gunshot wounds.
16 factories were burned down.
170 homes were wrecked.
24 Catholic pubs were destroyed.

1970
The IRA began a 'war' against the British army. The first British soldier was killed. Overall, 26 people were killed.

1971
186 killings, including 46 soldiers.
The IRA began a major bombing campaign. They had detonated 136 bombs by May. They targeted Protestant-owned shops and businesses.

■ ACTIVITY

In the diagram you can see the options facing the British and Northern Ireland governments in 1971.

1 How do you think **a)** Republicans and **b)** Unionists would react to each option?

2 Which option would you have chosen in 1971? Explain the main reasons for your choice.

The aim – to restore order and stop the violence as quickly as possible.

Option 1 – take the army out of Northern Ireland and rely on the police to keep order.

Option 2 – use the army and the police to arrest and then intern troublemakers. Internment means to imprison without trial. This method had worked against the IRA fifteen years earlier in 1956.

Option 3 – use the army and the police to arrest troublemakers, put them on trial and then imprison them if they are found guilty.

Option 4 – make an agreement with the Republic of Ireland that Northern Ireland should become part of the Republic as soon as possible.

Why did internment make peace more difficult?

The government of Northern Ireland decided to introduce internment in August 1971. The aim of internment was to stop the violence and eliminate the paramilitary threat. Over 2300 people were interned, but the information used to select these people was out of date. None of the new Provisional IRA leaders were interned and 1600 people were interned who either had never been involved in terrorist activities or were no longer involved. This was not the only problem with internment. There were five other major problems:

1 Only Republicans were interned. No Unionist paramilitaries were interned.
2 Torture and violence were used against some of the internees.
3 Catholics and Nationalists in Belfast and Londonderry built barricades around their home areas to stop attacks by Unionists. These areas became 'no go' areas, even for the police and army.
4 Support for the IRA increased among some Catholics.
5 Internment was criticised abroad. In the long term it helped increase US support for the IRA.

INTERNMENT – anyone suspected of terrorism could be arrested and held in prison without being charged with a crime or being put on trial. There was no limit to how long they could be held in prison.

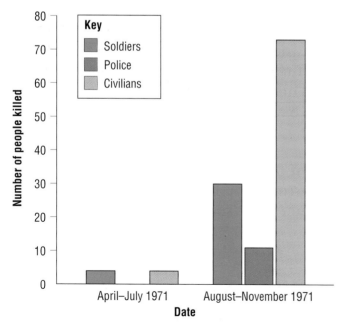

▲ **SOURCE 1** Deaths in the months before and after the start of internment in August 1971

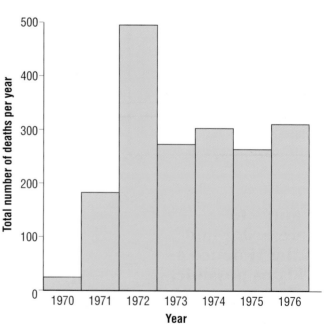

▲ **SOURCE 2** The number of murders in Northern Ireland, 1970–1976

■ **ACTIVITY**

1 Why did internment seem the most simple and obvious answer to the Northern Ireland government in August 1971? Look back to page 39 for ideas.
2 Internment did not make Northern Ireland more peaceful. Instead it made peace more difficult. Using the information on pages 40–42, copy and complete the table below with evidence to show the effects of internment.

Internment increased fear and resentment	Internment led to more deaths and violence	Internment increased support for paramilitary extremists

Bloody Sunday

On Sunday 30 January 1972 there was a huge protest march in Londonderry against internment. It was organised by the civil rights movement. Around 15,000 people met in the city, even though the march had been banned. Trouble began when the army cordoned off the area and were then stoned by local youths. Within minutes shots were fired. Thirteen marchers, all unarmed, were killed and another man died later as a result of his injuries. Some were shot in the back. There is still confusion over exactly how this happened and the event is still being investigated. Soldiers say they opened fire as they were fired at first. Source 4 gives a different reason.

▼ **SOURCE 3** John Hume's view of the effect of Bloody Sunday, 1972. Hume is a leading SDLP politician (see pages 12–13)

Many people down there in the Bogside now feel that it is a united Ireland or nothing.

▼ **SOURCE 4** An extract from *The Provos: IRA and Sinn Fein*, by Peter Taylor, a journalist with a lifetime's experience of reporting on Northern Ireland

To this day, it is difficult to convince Nationalists in the city [Londonderry] that the killing of their fellow citizens was anything other than premeditated [planned in advance] murder by the army, authorised by Stormont [home of the Northern Ireland Parliament] and the British government. How else, they ask, would soldiers slaughter thirteen innocent people taking part in a peaceful anti-internment march?

■ DISCUSS 1

The artist who made this mural wanted it to have a big impact on anyone who sees it. What message was the artist trying to get across? Do you think it is an effective mural?

▲ **SOURCE 5** A mural in Londonderry commemorating the victims of Bloody Sunday, Fahan Street, Derry

■ DISCUSS 2

Which of the following statements do you agree with?

A Internment was bound to make peace more difficult.

B Internment was a good, simple idea that would have reduced the amount of violence if it had been better planned.

Think about these points before you make your decision:

■ Would imprisoning people without trial be certain to lead to protests?

■ Could the police be trusted to use internment fairly against both Republicans and Unionists?

■ How easy was it to see the consequences of internment in advance?

■ Can simple ideas solve complicated problems?

Review: why don't the simple answers work?

The **big idea** in this chapter is:

The simple, obvious answers have often made peace more difficult because a complex problem needs complex answers.

In this chapter you have looked at three decisions:

1 1922 – Should Ireland be partitioned?
2 1969 – Should the British army be used in Northern Ireland?
3 1971 – Should internment be introduced to stop the violence?

In each case the decision led to more violence, even if, in the case of Partition, it took a long time to develop. Look at the reasons below. Which reasons help to explain the failure of each of the decisions on the left?

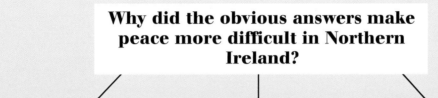

Why did the obvious answers make peace more difficult in Northern Ireland?

The obvious answers did not deal with the root of the problem, only the symptoms.

The obvious answers had unexpected consequences.

The obvious answers were not carried out properly as people were prejudiced and mistakes were made.

 using the big idea

What is in the news this week? Have there been outbreaks of violence in Northern Ireland – or in another part of the world?

Why don't they just . . .?

1 What kinds of simple, obvious answers are people suggesting to this problem?
2 Why might those simple, obvious answers lead to bigger problems in the long term?

Reason 1 – Separate lives

The main theme of this book is 'Why has it been so difficult to have a lasting peace in Northern Ireland?' Fears and prejudices are an important part of the answer, but why are fears and prejudices so strong? That is this chapter's big question. To answer it you need to firstly look at the everyday lives of Catholics and Protestants.

This street is like any other street – apart from the invisible wall down the middle of it. Can you work out why we have drawn the wall down the middle of the street?

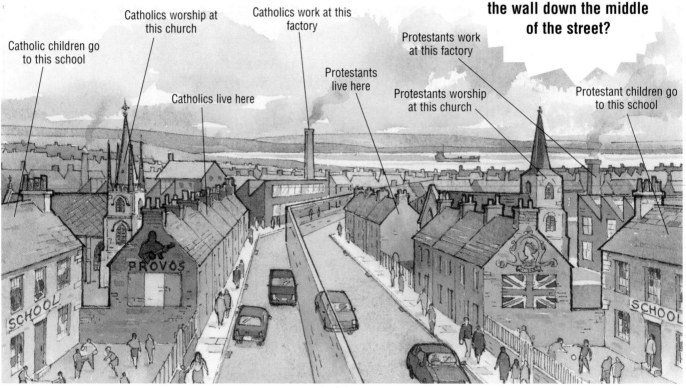

Catholic children go to this school

Catholics worship at this church

Catholics work at this factory

Catholics live here

Protestants live here

Protestants work at this factory

Protestants worship at this church

Protestant children go to this school

■ ACTIVITY

You are a journalist living in Northern Ireland, but today it's your turn to be interviewed – by an English journalist who has never been to Northern Ireland before. Use the sources opposite to help you answer his questions.

> I've heard that Catholics and Protestants did not mix together much during the Troubles.

> Did schools play any part in creating fear and prejudice?

> How about the Churches? Did they add to the fear and prejudice at all?

> What do you think are the effects of people living so separately?

> Did people mix more after they left school?

▼ **SOURCE 1** Dan Breen, a leading Republican in the nineteenth century, wrote:

My teacher did not just teach us history from the official textbook. He told us about the English conquest of Ireland and the way in which our country was held in slavery. He told us about the ruthless way in which Irish rebellions were crushed.

▼ **SOURCE 2** An extract from *No Surrender*, a book by Robert Harbinson, published in 1960. Harbinson was a Protestant who grew up in a Protestant area of Northern Ireland in the twentieth century

Our schools drummed into us over and over again the Protestant story. Our ignorance of the Catholic world was profound. I, for instance, believed that Mickeys [Catholics] existed only in parts of Belfast and nowhere else except the Republic of Ireland and Rome itself. It seemed impossible that many Catholics were living in London, or were allowed to live in London with our Protestant King.

▼ **SOURCE 3** An extract from *Reflections on a Quiet Rebel*, by Cal McCrystal, published in 1997. The author is a Catholic who grew up in Northern Ireland. He is now a journalist working in England

Prejudices were widespread among Catholics. They were narrowly dogmatic [stuck to their beliefs] and unyieldingly bigoted [prejudiced]. The Church was one source of this. Priests spoke about non-Catholics as though, if you were not a Catholic, you were nothing at all.

▼ **SOURCE 4** From a speech by Sir Basil Brooke, a member of the Unionist government who was Prime Minister of Northern Ireland in the 1950s

There are a great number of Protestants and Orangemen who employ Catholics. I point out that Roman Catholics are trying to get in everywhere. I appeal to Loyalists to employ Protestant lads and lassies wherever possible.

■ **DISCUSS**

1 What have you learned from these sources about why fears and prejudices are so strong?

2 When you have completed this chapter list three ways in which you think fears and prejudices could be reduced.

Reason 2 – The power of the paramilitaries

Now for another important reason why there is fear and prejudice in Northern Ireland. Can you help the English journalist again by answering some more questions?

PARAMILITARIES – organisations that are prepared to use violence to achieve their aims. There were Unionist and Republican paramilitaries operating in Northern Ireland.

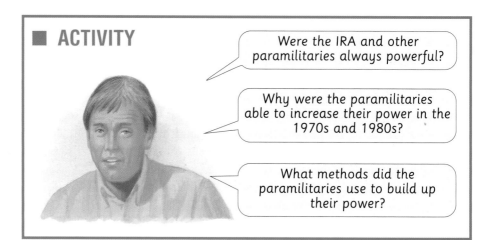

■ ACTIVITY

Were the IRA and other paramilitaries always powerful?

Why were the paramilitaries able to increase their power in the 1970s and 1980s?

What methods did the paramilitaries use to build up their power?

Paramilitaries in the 1950s and 1960s

▼ **SOURCE 1** An extract from an IRA journal, explaining why the IRA failed in the 1950s and 1960s

1 *People see no connection between the fight in the North and improving living conditions*
2 *A lack of money and weapons*
3 *A lack of good propaganda*
4 *A lack of public support so that we cannot keep a guerrilla war going*

Paramilitaries in the 1970s and 1980s

Until 1970 the IRA had little support because it did little to defend Catholics. However, in 1970 the Unionist government sent the army to search the Catholic Falls Road area. People were not allowed to leave their homes for 35 hours and tear gas was used to keep order. Suddenly the army looked like the enemy to many Catholics. At the same time, Catholic homes were being attacked by Loyalists. The Provisionals claimed that they could defend the people against the army and the Loyalists. Support for the Provisional IRA grew for the first time in many years.

▼ **SOURCE 2** An explanation from the *Irish Republican Information Service* of the disappearance of two men from a nationalist housing estate in Belfast, November 1974

Both men divulged a large amount of information, including the names and addresses of paid informers operating in Derry. Last night both men were executed.

▲ **SOURCE 3** A Provisional IRA checkpoint. These checkpoints were illegal. They were set up so that people could see that the IRA was taking action

▼ **SOURCE 4** An extract from a novel, *Lies of Silence*, by Northern Ireland writer, Brian Moore. In the novel, a married couple are held hostage by the IRA. The husband is forced to drive his car through security checks with a bomb in the boot, or his wife will be killed. Eventually he is killed by the IRA. This extract gives the wife's view of the IRA

If there was a vote tomorrow among the Catholics of Northern Ireland you wouldn't get five per cent of it. You're just a bunch of crooks, IRA or UDA, Protestants or Catholics, you're all in the same business. Racketeers [people who make money illegally and with the threat of violence], the bunch of you. There isn't a building site in this city or a pub that you or the UDA don't hold up for protection money ... You've made this place into a shambles and if it was handed over to your crowd tomorrow you wouldn't have the first notion of what to do with it ... You're not fighting for anybody's freedom. Not mine, not the people of Northern Ireland, not anybody's. The only thing you're doing is making people hate each other worse than ever. Maybe that's what you want, isn't it? Because if the Catholics here stopped hating the Prods, where would the IRA be?

■ DISCUSS

1 What opinion of the paramilitaries do you get from Source 4? Choose three words or phrases that sum up these opinions.
2 Source 4 is an extract from a novel. Can an invented story like this really help us to understand people's actions and attitudes?

Reason 3 – What's in, and isn't in, the news!

No more journalists – just newspapers! Do you think the news headlines help people live together more peacefully or do they lead to more fear and prejudice?

More death and hatred!

▶ **SOURCE 1** A bar in Loughinisland, County Down, in which six Catholics were shot dead by loyalist paramilitaries in 1994

▶ **SOURCE 2** The effects of an IRA bomb in Enniskillen, in 1987, which killed eleven people

■ DISCUSS

1 How would headlines and photographs such as Sources 1 and 2 affect the amount of fear and prejudice in Northern Ireland?
2 What effect might headlines and photographs such as Source 3 have on the amount of fear and prejudice in Northern Ireland?
3 Do you think that news headlines and stories are likely to increase or reduce fear and prejudice?

▲ **SOURCE 3** Lagan College, which was founded in 1981 to educate Catholics and Protestants together. The aim is to help people from different communities get to know each other

Living together in peace!

Causes

- living in separate areas
- going to different schools
- working in different places
- acts of violence
- the media focus far more on the problems than on examples of people living together in peace.

FEARS

pREJUDICES

Results

- paramilitaries find it easier to win support
- violence increases
- people move out of mixed areas and live in separate communities
- **it is far harder to get peace**.

The **big idea** in this chapter is:

One important reason why fears and prejudices are so strong is because of ignorance.

However, ignorance is the result of a mixture of different things and the cause of others. You can work out what they are from this Activity.

■ ACTIVITY

Draw your own vicious circle, using the boxes below, to show why ignorance led to fear and prejudice in Northern Ireland.

The actions of the paramilitaries increased people's fears.	Communities lived separate lives and were ignorant about each other.	The paramilitaries said they could defend their people against the other side.
This led to prejudice and fear between the communities.	Newspaper reports about the paramilitary violence increased the fear and ignorance between the communities.	

 using the big idea

What fears and prejudices are in the news this week? For example, when this book was being written, the papers were full of fears about asylum seekers. Fear of crime is also often in the news. Choose a story that is about people who are afraid of other people.

1 Who or what are people afraid of?
2 Why do you think this fear and prejudice has developed? (Use the ideas in this chapter to help you answer this.)
3 How could this fear and prejudice be reduced?

CHAPTER 5

Why should we be optimistic about peace?

■ ACTIVITY 1

1 Search the websites of newspapers such as the *Belfast Telegraph*, *Irish News* and *Irish Independent* to find headlines on the Troubles in Northern Ireland. Using the headlines you found as a guide, write a headline of no more than six words to go with each of Sources 1–4.

2 Which of the headlines/Sources 1–4 fit what people in England expect to see in their papers about Northern Ireland?

3 Which of the headlines/Sources 1–4 are very different from most news stories about Northern Ireland?

4 If you were making a TV documentary about Northern Ireland what music would you use as a soundtrack to the programme?

5 Read Source 5. Why do you think that many people in Northern Ireland are angry that most news is about violence?

▲ **SOURCE 1** The effects of a bomb attack in Omagh in 1998. The bomb was planted by a republican group who opposed peace talks. 29 people were killed

▲ **SOURCE 2** A peace march in Northern Ireland

▲ **SOURCE 3** Sinn Fein and DUP politicians at the start of the Good Friday Review in February 2004. These talks showed up deep divisions between the Nationalists and the Unionists, but at the same time, there had been no return to large-scale violence since 1998

▼ **SOURCE 5** A BBC journalist talking about TV and radio programmes in Northern Ireland in 1977, when there was a great deal of violence

In Northern Ireland, our extensive coverage of sport, musicians, writers and actors, the daily coverage of events in programmes such as 'Good Morning Ulster' and 'Taste of Hunni' are all about normal life. More than 80 per cent of Radio Ulster's output is about normal life.

▲ **SOURCE 4** Parents walk their children to the Holy Cross Catholic primary school in Belfast, under police protection, as Loyalists protest against Catholic children attending school in a Protestant area

■ ACTIVITY 2

'Six things about Northern Ireland that you never see on the TV news.'
As you go through this chapter, collect examples of people and events that show Northern Ireland is peaceful or that the people want peace. Then complete one of the following:
■ Write a list of six short points for an internet fact sheet on Northern Ireland.
■ Draw a series of cartoons showing peace or people's contribution to peace.
■ Search the internet for websites on tourism in Northern Ireland.

In 1998 the British and Irish governments and the politicians in Northern Ireland made an agreement about the future of Northern Ireland. This is known as the Good Friday Agreement. It set out plans to end the violence. Between 1998 and 2003 (when this book was written) Northern Ireland was far more peaceful, and hopefully it still is.

The **big question** in this chapter is:

Why should we be optimistic about peace despite all the violence in the past?

… because ordinary individuals can make a difference

The history of Northern Ireland features many heroes and heroines. Our 'Heroes and Heroines Gallery' contains some of the people who have taken positive action and helped others during the Troubles. Your task is to complete the gallery by writing the headlines and labels.

■ ACTIVITY

For our 'Heroes and Heroines Gallery', write:

a) A short caption of about ten words to go below each picture.

b) Up to 50 words explaining how each person or group made a difference to people's lives in Northern Ireland.
You could recreate our gallery using PowerPoint, adding your own images and even recording a commentary.

Heroes and Heroines Gallery

Betty Williams and Mairead Corrigan

Gordon Wilson

The ordinary people of Northern Ireland

Case study 1: Betty Williams and Mairead Corrigan – the Peace People

On 10 August 1976 an IRA getaway car crashed into Anne Maguire and her children. Three of the children were killed. Betty Williams, who had seen the crash, and Mairead Corrigan, Anne Maguire's sister, decided that they had to do something to try to stop the killings. They began a movement called the Peace People.

The impact of the Peace People

- 20,000 people attended a peace rally in Belfast, later in August 1976.
- 20,000 people joined a peace march through the loyalist area of the Shankill Road.
- 25,000 people joined a peace march through Londonderry.

At all of these meetings ordinary Protestant people talked to and walked with ordinary Catholics. They all wanted peace.

The Peace People also raised a lot of money. They used the money on community projects, helping ordinary people to improve their lives. In 1977 Betty Williams and Mairead Corrigan were awarded the Nobel Peace Prize. It was very unusual for two ordinary women to receive such a famous honour as it is usually given to politicians who have ended wars or worked hard for peace.

However, the Peace People could not bring an end to the violence. Many politicians and paramilitary groups opposed them. Loyalist politicians accused the Peace People of being on the side of the Republicans. Republicans argued that the Peace People were on the side of the British. By 1980 the Peace People movement had come to an end.

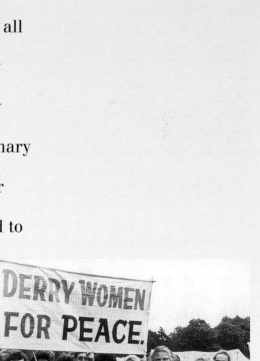

▲ **SOURCE 1** Catholic and Protestant women marching for peace in Northern Ireland, 1976

Case study 2: Gordon Wilson

In November 1987 Gordon Wilson and his daughter, Marie, were at the Remembrance Day ceremony in their home town of Enniskillen when an IRA bomb went off. Eleven people were killed, including Marie Wilson.

After the bombing, Gordon Wilson devoted his life to working for peace and bringing the two communities in Northern Ireland together. He played an important role in many peace groups and advised politicians on the best ways to bring peace. Above all, he was very critical of anyone who refused to compromise.

In 1993 Gordon Wilson was made a Senator of the Republic of Ireland in honour of his efforts to bring peace. When he died in 1995 there was a minute's silence in the Irish Parliament.

▲ **SOURCE 2** The scene of devastation at Enniskillen, 1987

▼ **SOURCE 3** Gordon Wilson's reaction to the death of his daughter

I bear no ill will. I bear no grudge. Dirty talk of that sort will not bring her back to life. She was a great wee lassie. She loved her profession [as a nurse]. She was a pet. She's dead. She's in Heaven and we'll meet again.

▼ **SOURCE 4** Part of a speech by Gordon Wilson in 1995

1690 was over three centuries ago: we are heading for the 21st century. Time has moved on. I appeal above all to politicians to stop playing politics with people's lives ... and to listen to what their grassroots supporters are saying. ... It seems to me that the man and the woman in the street are prepared to compromise.

Compromise is not giving in, it is maturity. I appeal to the political leaders to sit down, all of them, to listen to their electors ... to reach out to love their neighbours and their common God, and so to help us towards achieving peace.

Case study 3: The ordinary people of Northern Ireland

Many individuals have worked hard to put an end to the Troubles. They have not received much publicity because peace makes fewer headlines than violence. Here are some examples of community groups who have worked for peace.

The Ulster Project Northern Ireland

The Project's aim is to bring Catholics and Protestants together. It takes mixed groups of fourteen- and fifteen-year-olds to the USA. On these visits, the students socialise together and

come to realise how similar they are. Since the 1990s, 4000 students have taken part and not one has later become involved in paramilitary activities.

The Ballynafeigh Community Development Association

Local people formed this group to preserve their mixed community. They provide crèches, after-school activities and other practical resources to promote integration between local Catholics and Protestants.

Education

The Department of Education for Northern Ireland set up its EMU programme in the 1980s. EMU stands for Education for Mutual Understanding. This set up guidelines for teachers to help students understand and tolerate others. For example, History teachers would look at a balanced view of Irish history which would try to understand why Unionists and Nationalists sometimes have very different perspectives on events in Irish history. Many schools had developed EMU policies by the 1990s.

The Warrington Project

This project was set up in 1993 after a bombing in Warrington in Lancashire killed two young boys. It organises links between young people in Britain, Northern Ireland and the Republic of Ireland. It also publishes material for use in schools that helps students develop a better understanding of each other.

... *because other countries have helped to bring peace*

The Troubles are not just a British problem. Other countries, especially the USA, have also been closely involved. Your task is to complete the headline on the right summarising the USA's role in Northern Ireland.

▲ **SOURCE 1** In 1984 these weapons were found on a ship. They were being smuggled to the IRA from supporters in the USA

▲ **SOURCE 2** Two children introduce Bill Clinton, the then President of the USA, to a meeting in Belfast in 1995. The children were from local Protestant and Catholic schools

From ? to ?

In the 1970s the IRA received help from supporters in the USA. Perhaps as many as 80 per cent of the IRA's weapons came from the USA. An organisation called Noraid (Irish Northern Aid Committee) also collected and sent money from the USA to Northern Ireland. They said this was to help the victims of violence, but most of the money went to the IRA. However, the IRA's tactics eventually worked against them (see Source 3).

■ ACTIVITY 1

1 What can you learn about the involvement of the USA in Northern Ireland from Sources 1 and 2?
2 How would each kind of involvement affect the chances of peace?

▼ **SOURCE 3** The reaction of the *Chicago Tribune* newspaper to the IRA bomb in Hyde Park, London, in 1982

IRA front groups ... claim that they are raising funds for the families of slain or imprisoned IRA men. They lie. The money goes for arms, ammunition and bombs. It buys the high explosives and detonators that blew up in London. The money bankrolls the sort of sub-humans who can pack six-inch nails around a bomb and put it in a place where women and children and tourists will gather.

During the 1980s politicians who wanted peace were trying to win support in the USA. John Hume, the leader of the SDLP, worked hard to persuade US leaders to help bring peace to Northern Ireland. Bill Clinton was elected President of the USA in 1993. He took a leading part in bringing peace by:

■ holding meetings with politicians from all groups, including Gerry Adams of Sinn Fein. This gave Adams a stronger position in Sinn Fein from which he argued that the time had come for a ceasefire
■ promising that US companies would bring jobs and businesses to Northern Ireland once there was peace
■ visiting Northern Ireland several times to give his support to politicians working for peace
■ supporting US Senator George Mitchell who led the peace talks.

■ **ACTIVITY 2**

3 What did the help from the USA and the European Union have in common?
4 Why do you think John Hume and other politicians were so keen to get US help in bringing peace?
5 On a separate sheet of paper complete the heading on page 56. What words would you put into the blanks to describe the change in the USA's role in Northern Ireland?

The European Union has also done a great deal to bring peace to Northern Ireland. It has given £400 million to schemes to improve links between the different communities and to bring jobs to the area. It has also held meetings where politicians from the different sides have been able to meet and talk to each other.

... *because people can compromise*

The Good Friday Agreement, signed in 1998, led to a great reduction in violence, perhaps even to the end of the Troubles. Your task is to work out how all the people involved managed to reach an agreement after so many years of violence. You can do this by dismantling the 'Troubles Wall'.

Why did the Good Friday Agreement happen?

■ ACTIVITY

1 Your task is to take down the 'Troubles Wall'. You can do this by linking the people (in Box A) with the actions (in Box B) that they took to make the Good Friday Agreement possible. For every link you get right you can take one brick out of the wall. When you have got all the links then the whole wall has come down and the Agreement can be made.

2 Why do you think it was so difficult to reach the Good Friday Agreement?

3 In one sentence explain why the Agreement was possible.

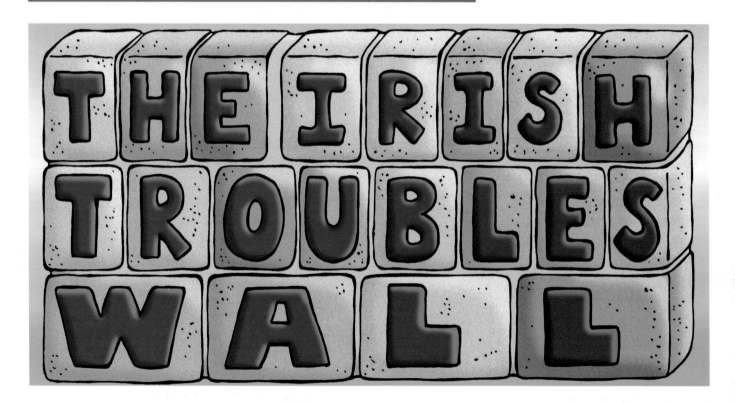

Box A

1 British politicians – John Major: British Prime Minister 1990–1997, Tony Blair: British Prime Minister 1997 onwards (4 links)

2 Irish leaders – Mary Robinson: President of Ireland 1990–1997, Bertie Ahern: Taoiseach (Prime Minister) of Ireland 1997 onwards (4 links)

3 US leaders – Bill Clinton (2 links)

4 Sinn Fein – Gerry Adams (2 links)

5 SDLP – John Hume (1 link)

6 Unionists – David Trimble (3 links)

7 Loyalist paramilitaries (2 links)

8 IRA paramilitaries (2 links)

Box B

a) agree to a ceasefire, end the attacks and killings

b) call off marches throughout Northern Ireland

c) agree to DECOMMISSIONING weapons

d) bring money and jobs to the area

e) put pressure on groups to meet and talk

f) lead the talks and show that you are determined to bring peace

g) accept that Northern Ireland will not become part of the Republic in the near future

h) accept that reforms are needed, for example, of the police force

i) agree to a Council that includes politicians from both Northern Ireland and the Republic of Ireland

j) agree to release paramilitary prisoners early

k) end your claim that Northern Ireland is really part of the Republic

l) convince the Republicans that they could achieve more by peaceful means than by violence

The Good Friday Agreement, 1998

The main terms of the Good Friday Agreement

1 A new Northern Ireland Assembly (Parliament) was set up. Major decisions must have the agreement of all communities.

2 A North-South Assembly was set up, including leaders from the Republic of Ireland and Northern Ireland.

3 The Irish Republic ended its claim to Northern Ireland.

4 The policing of Northern Ireland was to be reviewed to remove fear of anti-Catholic bias.

5 The British government promised to release paramilitary prisoners early.

In May 1998 a REFERENDUM was held in both the Irish Republic and Northern Ireland. All voters had the chance to say whether they agreed with the Good Friday Agreement. Source 1 shows the results.

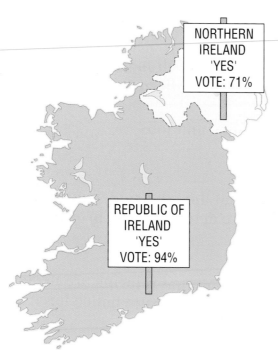

SOURCE 1 The results of the referendum on the Good Friday Agreement

SOURCE 2 Devastation caused by a bomb, planted in Omagh in August 1998 by the Real IRA (a splinter group of the IRA)

■ ACTIVITY

1 Look at points 2–5 of the Agreement. Who did each of these points try to please?

2 Look at Source 2. Why do you think some paramilitaries on both sides did not support the Agreement?

Review: why should we be optimistic about peace?

The **big idea** in this chapter is:

Despite all the violence, there are three good reasons to be optimistic about peace:

- Ordinary individuals can make a difference.
- Other countries have helped to bring peace.
- People can compromise.

This is how the situation has changed as a result of these three reasons:

■ **ACTIVITY**

1 How does Source 1 help to explain the changes that took place in Northern Ireland?
2 Which of the three reasons do you think is the most important for being optimistic about peace?

▼ **SOURCE 1** The view of a former IRA activist, Gabriel Megahy, in 1998

I'm prepared as a Republican to settle. My hopes are for the unification of this country, but I have to accept in the long run that it's not going to happen. The Brits are not going to sail away in the sunlight. Go back to war? What are we going to do? It would only cause more misery, more suffering and mostly to our own people and to ourselves.

using the big idea

The big idea in this chapter is that we have to be optimistic about peace. Choose another region of the world where there is violence. Can you use this chapter to think of reasons why the violence there might end?

We began with a set of questions:

What caused the Troubles? Is it really all about religion?

Does history really make peace more difficult?

Why are fears and prejudices so strong?

Why has it been so difficult to have lasting peace?

Should we be optimistic about peace?

Why don't the simple answers work?

And now we have some answers!

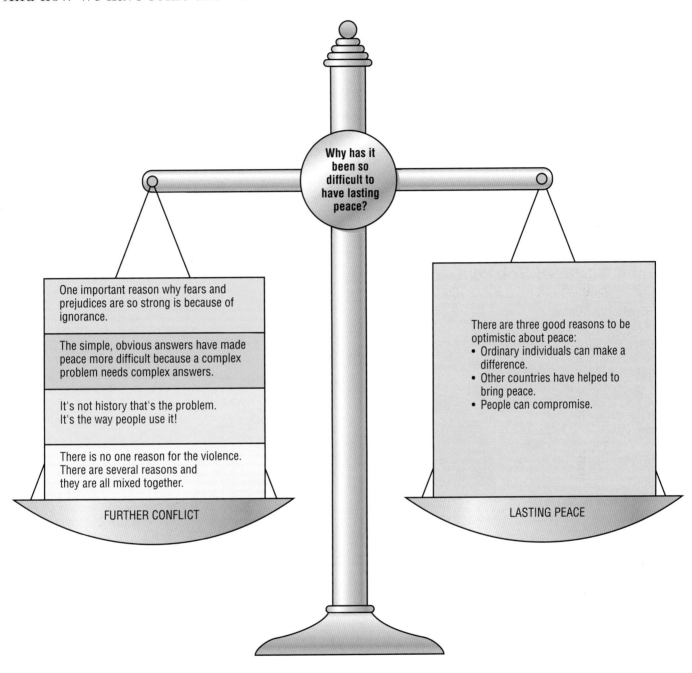

Why has it been so difficult to have lasting peace?

One important reason why fears and prejudices are so strong is because of ignorance.

The simple, obvious answers have made peace more difficult because a complex problem needs complex answers.

It's not history that's the problem. It's the way people use it!

There is no one reason for the violence. There are several reasons and they are all mixed together.

FURTHER CONFLICT

There are three good reasons to be optimistic about peace:
• Ordinary individuals can make a difference.
• Other countries have helped to bring peace.
• People can compromise.

LASTING PEACE

■ DISCUSS

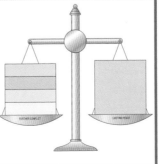

The scales on this page show a delicate balance between peace and violence. How do you think the scales should be drawn at the time at which you are studying Northern Ireland? Record your own views, then read the next two pages to see what others think.

Optimism or pessimism? Are Northern Ireland's troubles over?

■ ACTIVITY

This book was written in 2003. You will need to update yourself on key developments since then. Use a chart like this to record these developments and decide whether these events support the pessimists or the optimists on these two pages.

Key developments (with dates)	
Importance (based on points like the amount of media coverage, the impact on the peace process or on ordinary people)	
Supports the pessimist or optimist view (with explanation)	

The new Northern Ireland Assembly

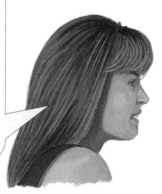

Optimistic view:
The Assembly first met on 1 July 1998. It appointed Lord Allardice as its Speaker, David Trimble as First Minister and the SDLP's Seamus Mallon as his Deputy. Northern Ireland politicians were in the same building, and arguing like normal politicians! All the major parties, even Sinn Fein, had ministers in Northern Ireland's government.

Pessimistic view:
The Assembly took a long time to agree who could be a minister. There were walkouts by some Unionist politicians over the lack of decommissioning by the IRA. In 2002 the Assembly was suspended after Unionists threatened to walk out because the IRA had still not given up its weapons. In 2003 the Unionists are continuing to demand the full decommissioning of the IRA, while Republicans are demanding that the British government should implement all of the terms of the Good Friday Agreement.

Paramilitaries

Optimistic view:
In the next few years we should see an end to political violence altogether. It must be hard for victims' families to watch prisoners being released early, but without releases it is hard to see how peace will last.

Pessimistic view:
First of all, there has been no decommissioning of any weapons. Secondly, paramilitary punishment beatings of people in their own areas has never stopped. And thirdly, the release of paramilitary prisoners is an insult to the families and loved ones of thousands of innocent victims.

Orange marches

Optimistic view:
Marches still cause some clashes every summer, but there are thousands of peaceful Orange marches and only about 50 are disputed.

Pessimistic view:
There is a core of loyalist hardliners associated with the Orange Order. These parades will continue to cause problems.

A divided republican movement

Optimistic view:
Gerry Adams and Martin McGuiness have won over most Republicans to a non-violent approach. The Omagh bombing of August 1998 was horrific and inexcusable, but it might be a turning point. Violent Republicans, like the Real IRA, have now been marginalised.

Pessimistic view:
There are still plenty of hardliners in the republican movement who will never accept anything but a 32-county Irish Republic. Also, public opinion in the Republic was appalled before, by Bloody Friday in 1972, and by Enniskillen in 1987. The men and women of violence will always find somewhere to hide. These extremists really believe they are right so they'll be back.

Security and policing

Optimistic view:
It might be said that in 1969 the RUC and B-Specials were often biased. Today's police force is professional and well disciplined. They stood up to the Loyalists at Drumcree in 1998. It changed its name from Royal Ulster Constabulary to the Northern Ireland Police Service in 2000 after the Patten Report.

Pessimistic view:
Drumcree has helped, but some Nationalists still don't trust the police. They remember internment and the allegations of human rights abuses. We should also remember that many Nationalists who try to join the police find that their families are intimidated by republican activists.

using the big ideas

This is how we began this book:

A Modern World Study does not just tell you what is happening today. It helps you understand why these things are happening.

By looking back into the history of Ireland you have seen how events that happened many years ago still affect what happens today. This is the history that lies behind the news. The more you find out about that history the more you understand the recent conflicts and why it has been difficult to achieve lasting peace.

To do this you asked and answered some big questions:

Is it really all about religion?
Does history really make peace more difficult?
Why don't the simple answers work?
Why are fears and prejudices so strong?
Why should we be optimistic about peace?

■ ACTIVITY

Now for a challenge. Here are two other news stories. You may not know anything about them yet. But now that you know how to do a Modern World Study how might you start to find out about the history behind these news stories?

Work with a group or a partner. Choose one situation only and then brainstorm questions which might help you get behind the news. Think about the questions you asked about Northern Ireland. Think about the big ideas (see page 63). Then write down as many questions as you can.

A Israel/Palestine

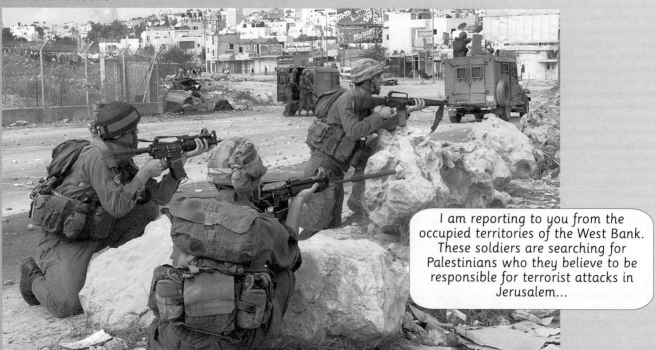

I am reporting to you from the occupied territories of the West Bank. These soldiers are searching for Palestinians who they believe to be responsible for terrorist attacks in Jerusalem...

B India/Pakistan

I am reporting to you from India where fans are celebrating the first visit by an Indian cricket team to Pakistan for fourteen years. It is a symbol of the lessening of tension between the two countries who have been at war for many years and indeed have come close to using nuclear weapons...

Using historical skills

In this study you have also been using some key historical skills:

Understanding causes – the complicated mixture of reasons that explain why things happen.

Comparing interpretations – and understanding why the same events can be interpreted in different ways.

Using evidence – and deciding which evidence to trust.

■ DISCUSS

Explain in your own words how these skills can be useful in studying events such as those shown in pictures A and B.

Glossary

B-SPECIALS part-time armed Special Police Constables who served in Northern Ireland from 1922 until 1970

CIVIL RIGHTS equal treatment for all citizens, whatever their religion, nationality or political beliefs

DECOMMISSIONING process in which paramilitary groups in Northern Ireland give up their weapons

DENOMINATION a religious group with its own particular beliefs, organisation and practices

GUERRILLA type of warfare involving hit-and-run attacks rather than open battles

HOME RULE measure to give Ireland its own parliament to rule itself, but leaving Ireland within the British empire

INTERNMENT policy of arresting and holding suspects without trial

LOYALISM / LOYALIST hardline Unionism – Loyalists are loyal to the monarch of the United Kingdom

NATIONALISM / NATIONALIST political view which wants a united Ireland free of connections to the United Kingdom

PARAMILITARIES violent republican and loyalist organisations

REFERENDUM vote on a key issue to see whether the population approves or disapproves of a particular action by the government

REPUBLICAN extreme nationalist political view, usually prepared to support force to achieve a united Ireland with no connection to Britain

TROUBLES term used to describe the conflict in Northern Ireland from 1969 onwards

ULSTER one of the four provinces which make up Ireland, consisting of nine counties

UNIONIST political view supporting the parliamentary union of Great Britain and Northern Ireland

Index